My First Ballet Book

KINGFISHER

a Houghton Mifflin Company imprint
222 Berkeley Street
Boston, Massachusetts 02116
www.houghtonmifflinbooks.com

First published in 2006
10 9 8 7 6 5 4 3 2

2TR/0307/LFG/CLSN/140MA/C

Copyright © Kingfisher Publications Plc 2006

All rights reserved under International and
Pan-American Copyright Conventions

LIBRARY OF CONGRESS CATALOGING-IN-
PUBLICATION DATA has been applied for.

ISBN-13: 978-07534-6026-9

Printed in China

Senior editor: Catherine Brereton
Coordinating editor: Caitlin Doyle
Senior designer: Peter Clayman
Photographer: Richard Brown (www.richardbrown.photographer.com)
Costume and hair stylist: Lindsay Jackson
Picture research manager: Cee Weston-Baker
Senior production controller: Jessamy Oldfield
DTP manager: Nicky Studdart
DTP operator: Claire Cessford
Consultant: Raymond Lukens

Girls' practice clothes and shoes supplied by
Gamba Dancewear, London, England
Now in Paris, France: Repetto Paris, rue de la Paix,
75002 Paris, France
Costumes supplied by Lindsay Jackson.

Children from The West London School of Dance:
www.thewestlondonschoolofdance.co.uk

Photographed at English National Ballet School:
www.enbschool.org.uk

Additional photography on page 32 and pages 42–45 by Joshua Tuifua at
The Royal Ballet, with kind permission of The Royal Ballet and dancers.

Note to readers: The web site addresses listed in this book are correct
at the time of going to print. However, due to the ever-changing nature
of the Internet, web site addresses and content can change. Web sites
can contain links that are unsuitable for children. The publisher cannot
be held responsible for changes in web site addresses or content or for
information obtained through third-party web sites. We strongly advise
that Internet searches are supervised by an adult.

My First
Ballet
Book

Kate Castle

Ballet direction by
Anna du Boisson

KINGFISHER

BOSTON

Nyack Library
59 South Broadway
Nyack, NY 10960

Contents

What is ballet?

Ballet is a special way of dancing onstage.
It is more than 400 years old and uses steps
and movements, music, scenery, and costumes
to tell a story and spark an audience's imagination.
The movements take a lot of practice to perfect,
but ballet is fun to do and spectacular to watch.

When two people
dance together
in a ballet, it's
called a pas de
deux or duet.

A ballet teacher
teaches the students
in a ballet studio.

Costumes help
create characters
in a ballet, like
these snowflakes.

Preparing to perform

These dancers are rehearsing for a production of *The Nutcracker*, a very popular ballet set to music by Tchaikovsky. It is often performed at Christmastime.

Toy story

The Nutcracker is about a girl named Clara who is given a magic nutcracker doll one Christmas. She travels to the Kingdom of Sweets, where she watches dances and meets the Sugar Plum Fairy.

Ready to dance

If you want to learn ballet, you will need to find a good school and a qualified teacher. Since your muscles and bones are still growing, you need to be taught correctly and safely. Dancing is a great way to exercise, and you will meet new friends.

Make sure that you come to class on time, wearing your practice clothes.

Be ready to listen to the teacher and dance your best.

Special clothes

You can buy ballet clothes and shoes at a dance store. You will need to buy the right shoes, and you can keep all of your equipment in a special ballet bag.

Top tip

Checklist

Remember to bring:

- ballet practice clothes
- ballet shoes
- a hairbrush and a comb
- for girls: bobby pins, elastic bands, and maybe a hairnet or a headband
- a bottle of water
- some fruits for energy
- a notebook and a pencil so that you can write down what you learn

What to wear

Ballet practice clothes are designed so that you don't get too hot and you can move easily. They are tight fitting so that your teacher can clearly see how your arms and legs are moving and can correct any mistakes. Many schools have special uniforms—one for girls and one for boys.

neat hairdo

leotard

practice skirt

Neat hair

Hair needs to be neat and brushed off your face so that the audience can see your expressions—and so it won't get in your eyes.

pink tights

Girls can braid their hair and put it up with bobby pins or elastic bands, use a headband, or pin their hair into one or two buns covered by a hairnet.

soft leather shoes

leotard or
T-shirt

Ballet shoes

Girls and boys wear soft ballet shoes
made out of leather or canvas for classes.
The shoes have elastic sewn on to stop
them from coming off. It's important to
make sure that the elastic is sewn on in
the right place—ask your teacher to
show you. Dancers often wear satin
shoes for performances.

Top
tip

Safety first!

Don't wear jewelry! It spoils the clear
shapes and lines that you are making
with your body and can be dangerous
if it gets caught on another dancer.

stretchy
shorts

Make sure that
the drawstrings
on your shoes are
tucked in neatly.

clean white socks

Ballet school

Ballet students and professional ballet dancers all practice in a studio like this one. There are wooden handrails, called barres, around the walls and mirrors so that you can check that your positions are correct.

What to expect
Every class begins with a warm-up, followed by exercises at the barre. Then you come together into the center and put the steps and movements together.

Top tip

Choosing a class
When you visit a studio, check whether:
- the students look like they're having fun
- there is enough room to dance
- the teacher is helping everyone learn
- the music makes you want to dance
- you can dance in recitals for friends and family

barre

This practice tutu is worn by older students when they learn to dance with a partner.

These students are warming up before class begins.

Your teacher

The teacher will have passed examinations, which means he or she is allowed to teach dance. Sometimes the teacher will have been a professional dancer in a ballet company.

Teamwork

You can help each other by watching and talking about ballet with your friends.

The teacher welcomes a new girl to the class.

The music

Without music, it would be difficult to dance in time— and a lot less fun! Some schools use a pianist to play for classes, while others use a CD player.

The special floor is not too hard or too slippery.

Warming up

All dancers need to stretch and warm up their muscles before they practice or perform onstage. This is to prevent injuries. At the end of a class they will also cool down.

In this exercise, you sit up tall and flex and point your feet in order to develop strong insteps, which you need for jumping and dancing on your toes.

Turning out

Ballet students learn to turn out their legs by moving their hip sockets so that their knees face the side, not the front. This means that they can raise their legs higher.

This Achilles stretch will help you jump higher.

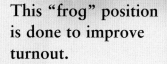

This "frog" position is done to improve turnout.

This exercise is for strengthening and loosening the inner thighs.

Get moving

After your stretches, it's time for some lively marching, skipping, and running. These exercises help your movements flow and get your whole body working together.

This position strengthens your back.

This position stretches the hamstring muscles at the back of your thighs.

Top tip

On your own

Practice at home— a little bit every day. You can also show your friends at school how to warm up before gym class.

• Back stretch
• Hamstring stretch
• Tendon stretch
• Skipping, running, and "pony trots"
• "Frogs" for turnout (ballet only)

first

second

Beautiful arms
Arms make clean,
curving shapes, so keep
your hands in line, not
drooping or sticking up
at an angle.

Here, all of the
students have their
feet in first position
while they demonstrate
the five different
arm positions.

Arms and feet

There are five basic positions for the feet
and five for the arms. These are used in
many different combinations to make
beautiful, expressive positions. All ballet
movements begin and end in one of the
five feet positions. Enchaînements use
traveling, jumping, and turning steps
in different combinations. Different
enchaînements make up the solos, duets,
and group dances that form a ballet.

Graceful hands
Your fingers
should be
held softly—
not in a fist
or straight out!

third   fourth   fifth

French words

Because ballet began in France, all of the steps have French names. These are the basic movements.

- plier—to bend
- tourner—to turn
- sauter—to jump
- relever—to rise
- glisser—to glide
- étendre—to stretch
- élancer—to dart

Neat feet

Although there are five positions for the feet, the ones that dancers use the most are second, fourth, and fifth.

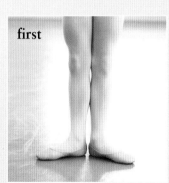

first

second

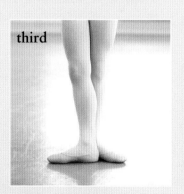

third

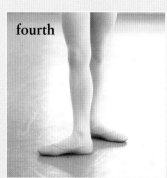

fourth

fifth

At the barre

The barre is your friend! It gives you support while you practice turning out your feet and legs. It helps you stand straight and tall with all of the parts of your body in line with each other.

Right and wrong

There are many things to remember when you are standing at the barre, such as: stand straight, stomach in, shoulders level, and arms and feet in the right place. Don't forget to breathe!

At the barre, don't grip or clutch the barre like this . . .

. . . but hold it lightly and firmly as if it's your partner.

To stand correctly, don't hunch your shoulders like this . . .

. . . but stand tall— stomach pulled in, shoulders down.

Point your feet neatly, not pressed out of line . . .

. . . but pointed like this, with your foot straight to the side.

★ Top
tip ★

Fun for all

Anyone can learn to enjoy ballet, although not everyone wants to be a professional dancer. Ballet is a great way to stay fit and healthy, build confidence, and develop your memory.

Demi-plié in first position of the feet at the barre, with the arm in second position.

Barre exercises

These students are stretching their feet in a movement called battement tendu devant. "Devant" means "to the front." They will also practice pliés (bending) and relevés (rises).

Relevé facing the barre. The children are rising with their feet in first, second, and fifth position.

19

Here to help
Your teacher helps with
turnout and alignment,
so by the time you dance
onstage, you won't
have to think about it.

Aiming higher

As you become older and stronger,
you will be able to do more difficult
exercises and feel like you are really
dancing. Even famous dancers still
do their warm-up and barre exercises
in a daily class that lasts for an hour
and a half, before they even begin
to rehearse or perform.

Arabesque penchée—
which means
"tipped"—with
the arm in
second position.

Arabesque
The arabesque is
a beautiful position
used in all ballets,
and there are many
different types.

Older girls do their exercises at the barre en pointe, like this relevé in the retiré position with the arm in fifth position (left).

They do more difficult warm-ups too, like this stretching exercise for the back and hamstrings (right).

First arabesque— notice the turnout of the dancer's legs.

Arabesque à terre— on the ground. The legs are not quite so turned out because this dancer is much younger.

Into the center

After the barre exercises, it's time to come into the center. The studio is like the stage. Center practice is about using the space so that the audience sees your dancing from the best possible angle. You face front, toward the audience.

In line

Exercises help you make beautiful shapes in the space around you. This is called "line" and means arms and legs making movements that relate to each other in a way that is pleasing to look at.

This girl is doing a first arabesque, facing the corner of the studio, not the front.

Top tip

Step by step

In the center, you'll learn:
- port de bras—flowing arm movements
- adage—slow movements for balance and stretching
- petit allegro—small, neat jumps
- grand allegro—large, traveling leaps

The girls in the center and right of the group are in croisé, or crossed, positions, with their bodies turned toward opposite corners of the studio.

You can turn your back on the audience if your position has line and expression.

1 The pas de bourrée is a linking step. Begin in fifth position of the feet and do a plié with your arms in first position.

2 Slide your left foot out to the side, moving your arms to second position. Don't forget to point your left foot.

3 Pull up into fifth position of the feet, in relevé, with your stomach in and your shoulders down.

4 Step to the side. "Pas" means "step." Remember to focus toward the direction that you are traveling in.

5 Close into a plié again, with your head facing left. The sequence ends when you straighten your knees.

Spread your wings

Once you move away from the barre and into the center, you can really fly! Jumping, turning, and traveling steps make ballet exciting to watch and fun to do. Practicing at the barre gives you the strength and power that you will need in order to do more difficult steps with ease.

Jumping high up in the air is called "elevation." It takes strength and skill to make a clear shape like this.

Jumps—big and small

This dancer is leaping across the studio in a traveling jeté—which means "to throw." You can have fun jumping and turning right from the beginning. Remember to point your toes as you jump.

1 This jump is called a petit changement, or "little change." Begin in fifth position and do a demi-plié.

24

Taking off!

Begin with these petits sautés, or "little jumps." Start and finish in a demi-plié position. As you jump, remember to point your toes, keep your arms in position, your shoulders down, and your body straight.

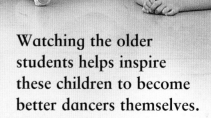

Top Tip

Up and down

Before you can go up in the air, you have to go down to the ground, so prepare for a jump with a good demi-plié. Don't throw your chest back as you jump, and make sure that you put your heels on the ground as you land. Try to land softly and quietly, not with a big thump!

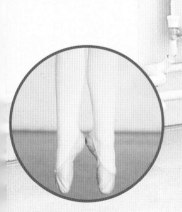

2 Jump in the air and change your feet, bringing the back foot to the front and pointing your toes straight down.

3 Land softly, and you've completed the changement. If you want, try doing several of these jumps in a sequence.

Watching the older students helps inspire these children to become better dancers themselves.

25

Spinning around

You can start to turn by skipping and turning while moving across the studio. It will take all of the skills that you have learned so far—keeping your head level, your arms straight, and your shoulders down while still breathing and smiling!

Stay focused

You need to focus when you do a skipping turn so that you don't get dizzy. Look at one spot and, just as you turn, quickly turn your head around so that you find the same spot again.

Top
tip

Ways to turn

You can turn:
- in soft shoes
- en pointe
- on the spot
- traveling on one leg
- supported by a partner

Why not try a spin yourself? Remember to focus on something so that you don't get dizzy.

Many turns

A dancer can learn many different types of turns, including pirouettes, piqué turns, and fouettés. The most difficult turns are the 32 fouettés danced by Odile in the ballet *Swan Lake*.

1 This is a pirouette en dehors (outward). The student is turning toward the leg that is in the retiré position.

2 Turns require precision. The dancer's leg is perfectly turned out so that her knee faces the side as she turns.

This dancer is in fourth position of the feet and third position of the arms, ready to push off into a fast spin or pirouette to her right.

This dancer is in the middle of a series of piqué turns. Solos in ballets sometimes end with a series of these turns, moving very quickly across the stage.

Dancing together

All ballets are made up of a combination of solos, duets, and group dances. In a solo, you dance alone; in a duet or pas de deux, you perform with another dancer. Large groups are called the corps de ballet.

With a partner

Dancing in pairs takes skill. You have to remember the steps while dancing at the same time as your partner and in time to the music. You need to show that you are enjoying dancing together, so making eye contact is important.

Keep your head straight as you dance shoulder to shoulder. Remember to point your toes as you skip!

This lift, called a pressage lift, is one of the most difficult in ballet, and it requires great strength.

Top
tip

Dance groups

- Solo—dance for one
- Pas de deux— dance for two
- Pas de trois—dance for three
- Pas de quatre— dance for four
- Corps de ballet— large group

Remember to point your toes, hold your stomach in, make the right shapes with your arms and legs—and smile!

Stay together

Watch the person next to you and try to keep perfectly together and in line when dancing this pas de trois—a dance for three.

This pas de deux is danced by older students. Use your finger to trace the lines and curves that the dancers make with their bodies in the space around them.

29

On your toes

Dancing en pointe—on the tips of the toes—is something that all young ballerinas look forward to. It makes turns look faster and more exciting, lengthens the legs so that positions look even more beautiful, and gives the impression that the dancer is very light, just skimming the ground.

Top tip

Safety first!

You can dance on your toes when:
- your legs and feet are strong enough
- your stomach muscles are strong enough
- you go to ballet class at least three times each week
- you are old enough (around 11 or 12)
- your teacher says you can

A lot of strength

It takes a great deal of practice before a dancer's stomach and leg muscles are strong enough for dancing en pointe.

Pointe shoes are special shoes that are stiffened with layers of material and glue and then baked hard. The tips are flat so that you can balance on them.

30

Girls only

Only female ballet dancers dance on their toes. They will do all the same exercises and steps that the younger girls learn, like relevés and arabesques, but en pointe.

If you are taught correctly, pointe shoes won't hurt your feet.

Pointe shoes need to be fitted correctly. A professional ballerina may use up to ten pairs of shoes every month!

Time to dance

Now the fun can begin! You know enough steps to enjoy that magic moment when the music, costumes, and movements come together to make a ballet. The journey from studio to stage has begun. Change your practice clothes for a pretty costume, put on your best satin shoes, and get ready to dance!

It takes years of practice to become a prima ballerina—the ballerina who dances the principal roles.

Teamwork

Ballet dancers know that they are part of a team. Teachers, choreographers, musicians, designers, and backstage staff are as important as the dancers, but they work behind the scenes.

Remember that even if you do become a star, you will still need your friends to dance with!

Tutus

Ballerinas' dresses are called tutus. They are made of layers of tulle (net material) sewn onto a bodice trimmed with beads, ribbons, flowers, feathers, or fake jewels. Designing and making tutus and headdresses demands great skill.

33

Top tip

Your ballet

First, choose your story. Then find the right music. Make up the steps, called choreography. Design the scenery, costumes, and makeup. You can draw posters to advertise your ballet, sell tickets, and make programs.

Music is used to create a mood or suggest a character and to paint pictures in the listener's mind. Listening will give you ideas for steps.

This class has decided to create a ballet about Alice in Wonderland.

Let's make a ballet

Most ballet schools put on recitals where you can show off what you have learned to friends and family. The audience will admire your skill, but above all, you will be able to make them feel happy or sad and tell stories with your dancing. You can make up ballets yourself and with friends, at home or in a ballet studio.

1 Invent steps for the story and characters such as bunny hops for the White Rabbit.

2 Design your costumes and props. Costumes need to suggest the character but must be easy to dance in.

3 Put the finishing touches on your costumes. Use makeup to create the White Rabbit's nose and whiskers.

4 Perform your dance to the class. Here, Alice meets the White Rabbit. What are they telling you with their dancing?

From studio to stage

This ballet school is going to perform a ballet based on a well-known story, Peter Pan. The teacher has chosen the music, decided who will dance each character or role, and choreographed the steps. It's time for rehearsals to begin.

These children (left) will be John, Michael, and Wendy, the characters who fly to Neverland with Peter Pan.

The students find out which parts they will dance in the production.

The pianist will help the students rehearse their steps and dances.

Peter Pan and the fairy Tinkerbell are rehearsing their roles. You can see from her expression that Tinkerbell is angry at Peter Pan.

These boys are warming up during rehearsals. Part of the fun of dancing in a ballet production is meeting dancers from other classes.

Props

The objects that dancers use onstage are called props—such as the teddy bear and sword used in this scene.

The teacher helps the children practice the steps until they get them exactly right.

Practice makes perfect

After learning the steps, dancers will have many rehearsals in a studio and onstage before the ballet is danced in front of an audience. The dancers must remember the steps and dance them accurately, with expression and energy.

1 The dancers' costumes have been washed and ironed and are ready for them to put on. The dancers help each other get changed, making sure that all fastenings are secure.

2 The soloists arrive, pick up their costumes, and get ready for the performance.

Ready to perform

There is one final rehearsal onstage in costumes, called the dress rehearsal. Then the ballet is ready to be performed onstage for an audience. The dancers get ready and warm up backstage, and at last the curtain goes up! It's normal to feel a little bit nervous onstage.

3 The dressing room is backstage at a theater. Neat hair is very important.

4 You need makeup, or strong stage lighting will make your features seem to disappear!

The performance

Peter Pan dances with Tinkerbell, while John, Michael, and Wendy look on. Each dancer is wearing a costume and takes up a position that suggests their character.

Top tip

Stage words

- Stage—where the ballet is performed
- Backstage—where the dancers get ready and costumes and scenery are stored
- Curtain—a piece of cloth that hides the stage
- Wings —where dancers enter and exit the stage

Famous ballets

There are many famous ballets to enjoy. Some are based on fairy tales and magic and others on stories and plays. They fill the stage with movement, color, and music to delight audiences in theaters all over the world. You can watch ballets on TV and DVDs as well as going to see a professional performance.

The Firebird
Margot Fonteyn dances the role of the Firebird in this ballet based on a Russian fairy tale.

Musical dance
Not all ballets tell stories. *Elite Syncopations* uses colorful costumes and ragtime music by Scott Joplin to suggest all sorts of different moods—such as a funny duet for a tall dancer and a smaller dancer.

You will enjoy the ballet much more if you read the story and listen to some of the music before you go.

Giselle
This early ballet tells the story of a girl who falls in love with a prince in disguise.

The Nutcracker
The prince dances a pas de deux with the Sugar Plum Fairy.

The Sleeping Beauty
Many fairy tale characters dance at Princess Aurora's wedding.

Swan Lake
The black swan, Odile, pretends to be the prince's true love, the white swan Odette.

The Dream
This ballet is based on William Shakespeare's play *A Midsummer Night's Dream*. Enchanted creatures meet to cast their spells.

Behind the scenes

A dancer's day begins with a class and ends with a performance. In between are rehearsals, costume fittings, and, for principal dancers, coaching sessions. In a ballet company, everyone is important and has a part to play in making sure that the performance is the best it can possibly be.

Dancers rehearse in a studio wearing practice tutus and wrap sweaters.

Taking care

All dancers learn to take care of themselves by eating healthily and getting enough rest. They also need to be organized—to make sure that they are always on time for class!

This dancer is checking her rehearsal schedule. She stays warm with leg warmers and a sweatshirt and has a bottle of water with her.

This dancer is wearing a leg warmer on her injured leg.

Top
tip

Hard work

Dancing is as demanding as any other sport. Injured dancers have physiotherapy or massages to help them recover.

Dancers usually put on their own makeup. For some roles, special makeup is designed as part of the costume, and makeup artists are needed.

The dancers' arms are in fourth position as they make a battement tendu devant.

Dancers break in new pointe shoes during rehearsal so that they are comfortable and not too noisy.

Costume staff handle and repair costumes. Each dancer must be careful not to spill anything on them and to hang them up neatly.

43

At the ballet

At last—after all of the preparation, it's time for the ballet to begin. Everything comes together—dancing, music, scenery, and costumes. So sit down, watch, listen, and enjoy as the curtain rises on the magical world of ballet!

The Sleeping Beauty

In this scene, the Lilac Fairy blesses the baby Princess Aurora at her christening, while other fairies and courtiers look on. The shapes lead your eye to the most important people in the group—the Lilac Fairy and the baby princess.

Top tip

Enjoying ballet

Ask yourself some questions while you watch the ballet. What role would I like to dance? Do I know the names of any of the steps? How does the music help tell the story? How does the choreographer use steps to make patterns? How did the ballet make me feel—happy, angry, or sad?

Before the performance, musicians take their seats in the orchestra pit, and the audience is seated. Then the ballet can start!

During the ballet, dancers watch a pas de deux from the wings as they wait to go onstage themselves. The audience sees it from a different angle.

At the end of the performance, dancers do a curtain call—their final curtsy and bow—and thank the audience for applauding.

Thank you!

Programs tell you the story of the ballet and about the dancers. People sometimes give dancers flowers to show that they enjoyed the performance.

Glossary

Adage (a-dahge)
Slow and sustained steps and movements that flow from one to the next.

Alignment
The relationship of one part of the body to another.

Arabesque (ara-besk)
A position where a dancer balances on one leg with the other stretched out and raised behind him or her.

Barre
A wooden rail that is attached to the walls of a dance studio. Dancers use it for balance as they practice basic exercises.

Choreographer
The person who has the idea for a ballet and then arranges the steps and patterns so that they make a complete dance.

Corps de ballet (core duh ba-lay)
Dancers who perform together as a group and do not dance solos or leading roles.

Enchaînements (on-shane-mon)
A series of steps linked together, like words making a sentence.

En dehors (on day-or)
Outward from the supporting leg.

En pointe (on pweh)
Dancing on the tips of the toes in special stiffened shoes.

Étendre (eh-ton-druh)
To stretch.

Fouetté (fwe-tay)
A turn in which the working leg turns in a circular movement away from the supporting leg.

Glisser (glee-say)
To glide.

Grand allegro (gron a-leg-row) Large jumping and traveling steps.

Grand jeté (gron jeh-tay)
A large traveling jump, with legs and arms outstretched.

Hamstring
One of five tendons at the back of the knee.

Line
The graceful shapes made by dancers' bodies in the space around them.

Orchestra pit
Where the musicians sit to play and the conductor stands to direct them during a performance.

Pas de bourrée (pah duh bou-ray)
Series of small, linked traveling steps.

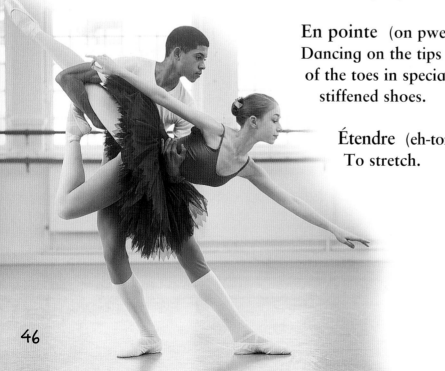

Pas de deux
(pah duh der)
A dance for two people
in ballet.

Pas de trois (pah duh
twa) A dance for three
people in ballet.

Petit allegro
(puh-tee a-leg-row)
Small jumping
and traveling steps
performed in
enchaînements.

Plié (plee-ay)
A basic ballet movement
in which the knees bend
and face the sides, not
the front.

Props
The objects that dancers
hold in their hands
onstage, which are kept
in the wings during
a performance.

Recital
A performance by
a ballet class in front
of an audience.

Rehearsal
A practice session before
a performance.

Relevé (reh-leh-vay)
To rise onto the ball
of the foot.

Role
The part or character that
a dancer plays in a ballet.

Sauter (soh-tay)
To jump.

Solo
A dance for one person.

Studio
The room where
you learn to dance,
have daily classes,
and rehearse.

Turnout
The way that a dancer's
legs turn out from the hip
sockets so that the knees
face the side.

Tutu
The ballerina's skirt, made
of many layers of gathered
net (tulle), which can be
very short (classical) or
calf length (romantic).

Wings
The space on the sides of
the stage that the audience
can't see, where the
dancers wait to come on.

For more information
about ballet, go to:

School of American Ballet
www.sab.org

American Ballet Theater
www.abt.org

And for performances of
ballet and other forms of
dance, contact your local
theater or dance agency.

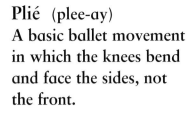

Index

Acknowledgments

The publisher would like to thank the following for their help in the production of this book:

Dancers: Leah Andreas, Curtis Angus, Helena Clark-Maxwell, Finn Cooke, Moesha Lamptey, Charlotte Levy, Helena Pratt, Kingsley Wong

The West London School of Dance: Kirsty Arnold, Anna du Boisson, Lindsay Jackson

English National Ballet School: Sue Preston

Photography: Richard Brown (www.richardbrownphotographer.com)

The Royal Ballet: Joshua Tuifua (photography), Lauren Cuthbertson, Victoria Hewitt, Jonathan Howells, David Makhateli, Kristen McNally Samantha Raine (dancers), Melanie Bouvet (ROH wigs/makeup), Alisa Woodyard (ROH costume)

Also: Ann Burke, Vicky Bywater, Claire Cessford, Sheila Clewley, Russell Mclean, and Jonathan Williams.

The publisher would like to thank the following for permission to reproduce their material. Every care has been taken to trace copyright holders. However, if there have been unintentional omissions or failure to trace copyright holders, we apologize and will, if informed, endeavor to make corrections in any future edition.
Pages 28*br* Alamy/Jeremy Hoare; 32*bl* Joshua Tuifua; 40*cl* Corbis/Robbie Jack; 40*tr* Getty/ Barron; 41*tl* Getty/AFP; 41*tlc* Topfoto/Performing Arts Library; 41*trc* Corbis/Robbie Jack; 41*tr* Corbis/Robbie Jack; 41*cr* Corbis/Robbie Jack; 42–43 all images Joshua Tuifua; 44*tr* Joshua Tuifua; 44–45*b* with the kind permission of English National Ballet, London, England; 45*l&r* Joshua Tuifua